If I Were Starting My Family Again

D0563202

If I Were Starting My
Starting My

John M. Drescher

illustrated by
Nancy Johnstone

Family Again

ABINGDON *Nashville*

If I Were Starting My Family Again

A Festival Book

Copyright © 1979 by Abingdon

Festival edition published October, 1981

ISBN 0-687-18674-9

Printed in the United States of America

Contents

I drank as deeply from this book as if it had been a crystal glass filled with sparkling clear water!

As a woman, wife, and mother I was thrilled beyond belief that a man, husband, and father had written so lovingly of the changes he would make in *his* life if he were starting a family again. (Does he have an unmarried brother or two just like him?)

I've talked with women all over the world who long for their husbands to take over the psychological and spiritual headship of their homes. This book by John Drescher could be a very important first step in that direction for any father. It conveys gently and with great humility the lessons life has taught one man about fathering and shows how the wisdom he has gained can be applied to the lives of other fathers.

If I Were Starting My Family Again is a refreshing treasure I know you'll enjoy.

Joyce Landorf

"What have you learned from your own experiences and from counseling parents? What should I have done differently? I have young children. If your children were small again, what would you do?"

These words burst from the burning heart of a father sitting across from me. His eyes pleaded for help. He was suffering the awful, empty, death-like feeling a father senses when his son has strayed. He felt he had failed as a father.

And this father's words stay with me. Although they came to me in a direct, blunt way that day, they are not the words of a lone parent. In them are the questions that are uppermost in the mind of all parents who take parenthood seriously.

What has experience taught me? What has

some experience in counseling given me? What insights and feelings might I have gleaned? And where would I place the emphasis if my children were small again? I've pondered these questions, and some things keep coming to the surface.

In answer to the father who sat across the desk I've jotted down my reflections. I've added a thought or paragraph now and again as it has come to me. Like most important experiences in life these ideas are not new or great. Nor are they difficult to remember.

These simple suggestions, however, I believe can make relationships with our children more meaningful and help shape the future of our children more than big things that demand a great deal of time and exceptional ingenuity. They are things that God has made so simple that all parents can practice them if they will.

What I am sharing here is what I wish I had realized more fully at the start of my own family. They remain goals toward which I seek to move. And if what is shared here can be even a small stimulus to parents just beginning or become a help in spurring on some whose families need a fresh nudge, my purpose will be fulfilled.

If I Were Starting My Family Again

I Would Love My Wife More

If I were starting my family again, I would love the mother of my children more. That is, I would be freer to let my children know that I love their mother. It is so easy, in the closeness of family life, to assume love, to take one another for granted, and so let a dullness creep in that can dampen the deepest love.

After I spoke on family relationships to a large group of parents, a father said to me, "If I understood you this evening, you said the greatest thing I can do for my child is to love his mother. Is that correct?" "Yes," I replied, "you are right. And the greatest thing a mother can do for her child is to love her husband."

When a child knows parents love each other, there is security, a stability and a sacredness about life that is gained in no other way. There is also a joy in relationships that is realized by no other means. A child who knows his parents love each other, needs little explanation about the character of God's love or the beauty of sex. And when mother and father smile in love, the child will smile back, and he will smile at the world around him. The love he feels between father and mother flows freely to him and prepares him to understand how to recognize real love in all future relationships.

To let my child know I love his mother I would seek to be more faithful in doing little things for her. True love is visible. I would show special kindnesses such as opening the car door for her, placing her chair at the table, giving her little gifts on special occasions, and writing her love letters when I'm away from home. I would take her hand as we stroll in the park or woods. And I would whisper loving words about her in the ears of my children.

To show my love I would seek more special times to be together with my wife. I remember the times the two of us went out, for a dinner or concert or to relax for an evening by the lake. That love shared by us alone was not felt by us only. When we returned, the children had sometimes decorated the dining room table or placed a large sign, Welcome Home, to greet us or arranged a short skit to perform. They felt a love between father and mother that they sought to share in.

I remember also when, as the children became older, they planned special times when their mother and I could take a break from the busyness and burdens of work and spend time together. "You and mother go away tonight, and we will stay at home," they said.

I now see more clearly than ever that when the child sees a close relationship of love between mother and father his love is enlarged and the best of life's joys and pleasures are pondered and produced. I'm persuaded that probably nothing gives a child so great an inner bubbling of joy and peace as when he feels and sees parents' love for each other, while the child who lives in conflict or in the suspicion that parents do not love, develops ulcers and bellyaches.

I now know that there is a close relationship between parents' love for each other and the child's obedience, love, and caring. When mother and father join hands as they walk, the child also joins hands. And when the mother and father walk separately, the child is slow to join hands with anyone.

I know that parenthood is passing. Children will soon be grown and gone. But the partnership of husband and wife is permanent. Therefore the courtship must continue. If we keep the permanent in good repair and growing, the passing will take care of itself. But if we fail in the partnership of marriage, the problems of parenthood become almost insurmountable.

Does all this sound too sentimental? Then I'm persuaded that we need a lot more of such sentimentalism. A big part of the problem is that often there is too much sentiment before marriage and too little following marriage. And there is no other thing that is more important for the future well-being of parent or child than the deep, abiding, visible love of father and mother for each other.

I Would Laugh More with My Children

If I were starting my family again, I would laugh more. That's right, I would laugh more with my children. Oscar Wilde wrote, "The best way to make children good is to make them happy." Charles Buxton wrote: "The first duty to children is to make them happy. If you have not made them so, you have wronged them. No other good they may get can make up for that."

I see now that I was, many times, much too serious. While my children loved to laugh, I, too often, must have conveyed the idea that being a parent was very painful and a perennial problem. Many families lose the ability to have fun, to laugh, and to play together.

I remember when I laughed with my children at the humorous plays they put on for the family, at

the funny stories they shared from school, at the times I fell for their tricks and catch questions. I recall clearly their squeals of delight when I laughed with them and shared in their stunts on the lawn or living room floor. And I remember the times they told of funny experiences the family had, years later. The stories were told with laughter and joyful expression, and I know it is the happy experiences that are remembered and still bind us together. I know when I laughed with my children our love was enlarged and the door was opened for doing many things together.

I remember how we laughed while traveling in the car. Seldom, if ever, did we need to scold when we were relaxed enough to laugh. I remember the time when we traveled through Nebraska when the temperature was one hundred degrees. We stopped for our lunch near a small but beautiful waterfall. After lunch the children waded into the stream, getting closer and closer to the falls. Finally, near the falls, one slipped and fell into the water. We laughed. All the clothes were wringing wet. Then another ventured near, and his clothes were soaked. Again we laughed. Finally the children sat under the falls itself, allowing the cool, clean water to pour down over their bodies. Then their clothes were changed. And today, after the years have gone by, that is one of those happy recollections.

An old sage said it rightly: "Never fear spoiling children by making them happy. Happiness is the atmosphere in which all good affections grow —the wholesome warmth necessary to make the heart blood circulate healthily and freely; unhappiness—the chilling pressure which produces here an inflamation, there an excresence, and, worst of all 'the mind's green and yellow sickness'—ill-temper."

So if I were starting my family again, I would laugh more at myself, my mistakes, my failures. So many of the tensions of life, particularly in the family, arise because we take ourselves so seriously. Then we can be hurt too easily.

I now believe that there needs to be the intermingling of work and play and laughter. And when we learn to laugh together we also learn to love and work together. If the important things of life are experienced by the child in the atmosphere of joy, he will not be as easily drawn to the frivolous or worldly fare by its blinding lights and suggestions for happiness.

Fénelon wrote many years ago: "Beware of fatiguing them by ill-judged exactness. If virtue offers itself to the child under a melancholy and constrained aspect, while liberty and license present themselves under an agreeable form, all is lost, and your labor is in vain."

"Blessed," says Douglas Jerrold, "be the hand that prepares a pleasure for a child, for there is no saying when or where it may bloom forth."

I Would Be a Better Listener

Most of us, as parents, find it hard to listen. We are busy with the burdens of what must be done. We are often tired when we arrive home from the job or from a full day's work of decision-making. We want to forget about things. Or we are wrapped up in our own interests and have little time to listen. A child's talk seems like unimportant chatter. Yet we can learn so much more by listening than by talking—especially from our children.

So, if I were beginning my family again, I would seek to be a better listener. I would listen when my child shares his little hurts and complaints, his joys, and what he is excited about. I remember, as clearly as the day it happened, the time my busy father listened to me as a first-grader when I came

home frightened by a situation in school. His calmness and concern, demonstrated by his listening to me, relieved my fears. I can no longer remember what the fears were. But I only remember sharing them and found it true that "fears talked about lose their power." I was ready to return to school the following day, full of fresh courage and confidence. Had my father simply said my fears were foolish or refused to hear me out, my fears would have grown.

If my child were small again, I'd stop reading the newspaper when he wanted to talk with me. And I would try to refrain from words of impatience at the interruption. Such times can be the best opportunities to show love, kindness, and confidence.

One evening a small boy tried to show his father a scratch on his finger. Finally, after the boy's repeated attempts to gain his father's attention, the father stopped reading and, impatient with the interruption, said, "Well, I can't do anything about it, can I?" "Yes, Daddy," his small son said. "You could have said 'Oh.'"

In listening I would pay more careful attention to my child's questions. It is estimated that the average child asks five hundred thousand questions by the age of fifteen. What a privilege for parents—a half million opportunities to share something about the meaning of life.

The early years are for teaching. And by the time the child reaches fifteen years, parents have done most of their teaching. That is, by the age of fifteen the child knows what parents believe. From then on the parents' responsibility is to be available when the child comes for advice or help.

If I had a chance to start over, I would listen more with the "third ear." I'd seek to hear what my child was feeling if he asked questions or made statements. If my child asked, "Daddy, must you go away again tonight?" I would hear him saying, "I want to be with you, Daddy." I would pay particular attention to the times my child might climb on my knees and share the happenings of the day. Those days of holding and listening are too soon gone. Jean Jacques Rousseau wrote, "The training of children is a profession, where we must know how to lose time in order to gain it."

Also I would keep from staring into space if my child were talking to me. I would stop and look into his eyes as I listened. Eyes reveal so much beyond words. It is a pity when a child needs to take his parent's face and turn it toward his own because he knows his parent is not listening.

I stood by the side of a father while his small boy called to him again and again. Seeing that I had noticed his son's calling and his not answering he said, "It's only the kid calling." And I thought, it will not be long before the father will call the son and his son will say, "It's only the old man calling."

I now believe that the parent who listens to his child in the early years will find that he will have a child who cares what his parent says later in life. I now believe there is a vital relationship between listening to the child's concerns when he is young and the extent to which the child will share his concerns with his parent when he is in his teens. I now believe that the parent who takes time to understand what his child says and feels early in life will be able to understand his child later in life.

I Would Seek to Be More Honest

If I were starting my family again, I would seek to be more honest. When I say that, I feel strange because I've always put a premium on being honest. I've always considered myself honest in the sense that I wouldn't keep a nickel that didn't belong to me nor would I knowingly tell a lie. I would not purposely misrepresent anything.

Yet I know from personal experience that parents practice many times another type of dishonesty that is more subtle yet very damaging. It is the dishonesty that pretends perfection or implies that one's own conduct as a child was beyond reproach.

One father confessed that he did not realize how dishonest he was until he learned a hard lesson.

His fourth-grade son received a very low mark in spelling. In spite of scoldings and extra study it seemed his son simply could not bring up his grade. One day the lad told his teacher, "When my Dad went to school he got all A's in spelling." "How do you know?" the teacher asked. "Did he tell you he did?" "No!" the boy replied, "but I know he did by the way he scolds me."

"In the way I scolded my son," the father said, "I conveyed an untruth. The fact is that I too had a hard time in spelling. I told my son I also had a difficult time in spelling. Immediately I saw hope shining in his eyes. From that moment on my son did much better. By giving him the impression I got all A's he felt defeated and hopeless. By being honest myself he had hope that since Dad made it he could too."

The way parents speak of their past or the "good ol' days" can cast reflection on the character, worthiness, and adequacy of their children. Children get hope from the confession that their parents fought similar battles and temptations. They love and respect parents who are honest with them. And the children will triumph.

Particularly when a child is discouraged it is necessary that parents be honest in sharing their defeats as well as victories, their failures as well as successes. When the child can feel that Dad and Mother had the same problems and see that they

are strong, there is new confidence and strength in the child.

I would seek to be more honest if my child came saying, "Daddy, I'm scared of the dark." To say "Don't be silly, don't be afraid," or to reprimand the child for his fear only harms the sense of inner strength that every child needs. To say, rather, "Son, when I was your age, I was also afraid," gives the help the child needs and builds confidence.

I do not mean by this that a parent should share all the failures of the past. Some parents even brag about past episodes and escapades of wrongdoing. This can only be harmful, of course. But to admit to a child that his problems are not unique since you also faced them is to give hope and to help in meeting life's difficulties. For any child to realize that his father, whom he should admire, fought the same battles is to give new courage and to evoke victory already existent in the heart and mind.

As long as parents pretend to be perfect and do not admit mistakes, the child lives in a world in which he is conditioned to failure and inadequacy.

I know now that the well-adjusted, happy child does not come from a home where everything is perfect or from the home that made the least mistakes. He comes from a home where parents made many mistakes but were honest, open, and loving enough to admit them.

I know now that a child who grows up in a home

where there is a great deal of arguing is better off than the child who lives in a home with Mother and Father who have inner hostilities, yet on the surface pretend all is fine for the sake of the child. The child senses hostility easily and does not know how to deal with it when it remains hidden. A child can deal with expressed hostilities only if they are followed by open expressions of love and forgiveness.

I know now that to demand exactness by implying that we ourselves never let tools lie on the ground, never cheated in an exam, or ever failed our parents can lead the child to feelings of insignificance and insecurity.

Yes, if I were starting my family again, I would seek to be more honest.

I Would Stop Praying for My Family

Does it sound strange or wicked to say I would stop praying for my family? Here is what I mean.

When I stopped praying *for* my wife and children great things happened. I began to see them in a new light. They became real persons. And it became easier to love them in spite of their faults. Mistakes took a minor role in relationships. In short, my own attitudes changed.

Often in the past I prayed prayers like: "Lord, help my son to be a good boy. Change his attitudes, Lord. Help him to a double dose of divine love. May he be more pleasant in all our family relationships. Help him to be obedient."

For my daughter I prayed that she might know Christ's love and also discern as she grows to ma-

turity what true love is in every relationship.

And for my wife I prayed that God might give her strength for all her duties in the home. I prayed that she might have plenty of patience with the children and that she might get done all that should be done to keep our home going smoothly. I prayed that as a busy mother she might have extra helpings of grace.

Then one evening it happened. I was alone when suddenly it struck me that this kind of praying must stop. It seemed my prayers really didn't help. If anything, the children knew less about love than they did in their earlier years. Traits such as caring and kindness were decreasing. And I realized I must stop praying for them. I was praying for the wrong person.

So I stopped praying like that for my family. I realized that if my children were to know Christ's love, then I, as their father, needed to experience more of Christ's love and make that love visible. If they were ever to learn true love in relationship to others, then I needed divine aid to demonstrate true love in all my relationships with my family and others. So my prayers turned to "Lord, make me fit to live with, loving, and kind, as you are to me."

I stopped praying solicitous prayers for my wife when I realized that my job was not to make her good but to make her happy. My prayer should not be for God to help her get all her work done. It should be to ask God to help me see those places where I could help her and make it easier for her. My prayers now turned to "Lord, make me a real husband, eager and happy to do all I can to make my wife happy." I realized I was the one who needed extra helpings of God's grace.

And you know, from that night on, my world changed. My home changed. It suddenly seemed that my wife and children changed. A new atmosphere of love pervades the house and even the car when we go driving. The children seem kinder. And it all started when I stopped praying for them and began to pray for God to give me a new attitude; when I asked God to help me refrain from all that might hurt those I love or hinder relationships; when I told God that I wanted to do all within my power to do what needs to be done to make my children and wife happy. Something happened when I wanted God to change me more than I wanted him to change other persons.

No, it hasn't all been perfect. I goof and I'm sorry. But I've learned that my family loves me right through my mistakes.

Of course, I still pray. My wife and children are as much in my prayers as ever. But now my prayers are primarily prayers of thanksgiving for each member of my family. And I believe that God desires this kind of praying because it also honors him who gave each one to me.

Yes, life really took on a new meaning and happiness when I stopped asking God to change others and asked him to change me.

I know now that when I accept my family for the persons they are, there are all kinds of possibilities for growth and change. But as long as I want to make them over or have God make them over, there is only resistance and propped feet.

I know now that when I have come to accept myself in God's eyes of love and forgiveness and in my own eyes that it is easier to accept others with a heart of love, overlooking their failures, and without the cruel condemnation that only kills.

I know that it is only as I, a parent, experience God's love that I am able to share that love with my family. Therefore, my prayers, when it comes to changing persons, need to be for myself. It is not my job to make others good. That's God's job. My job is to make others happy.

I Would Try for More Togetherness

If I were beginning my family again, I would try for more togetherness. It may sound strange to say to families who live, eat, and sleep together that they should try for togetherness. But many who live in the same house are worlds apart. And if there is one expression I've heard in family retreats and conferences over the years more than any other, it is "If I had it to do over I would spend more time with my children." These times together, not the things done alone, are what we remember.

In every father's week there are one hundred sixty-eight hours. He probably spends about forty hours at work. Allow another fifteen hours for driving to and from work each week, overtime, and lunch. Set aside fifty-six hours per week for sleep. This leaves a father fifty-seven hours each week to spend elsewhere. How many are actually spent with the family?

A group of three hundred seventh- and eighth-grade boys kept accurate records on how much time their fathers actually spent with them over a two-week period. Most saw their father only at the dinner table. A number never saw their father for days at a time. The average time father and son were alone together for an entire week was seven and one-half minutes.

A man tells an interesting experience from his youth: "When I was around thirteen and my brother was ten, Father promised to take us to the circus. But at lunchtime there was a phone call; some urgent business required his attention downtown. My brother and I braced ourselves for the disappointment. Then we heard him say, 'No, I won't be down. It will have to wait.'

"When he came back to the table Mother smiled, ' The circus keeps coming back you know.'

" 'Yes, I know,' said Father, 'but childhood doesn't.' "

A prominent businessman asked a friend, "Would you like to know what I am giving my son for Christmas?" He pulled out a piece of paper on which he had written, "To my Son, I give you one hour of each weekday and two hours of every Sunday to be used as you wish."

Today, I remember the times together I had with my father when I was a boy. The things I did

alone are largely forgotten. But the days we went together to the park, the times we ate a picnic together, and the visit together to a museum are cherished childhood memories.

One night I was about asleep when I heard footsteps in the hall. Three-year-old David came slowly through the doorway and stood by my bed.

"What do you want, David?" I asked.

"Nothing, Daddy," he said. "I wanted to crawl in beside you and talk a little."

I pulled the covers back and in he came. He snuggled there in silence a short time and then said, "Daddy, it was fun holding your hand in front of that lion's cage."

"It sure was," I answered. "Were you scared?"

"Just a little bit," he replied.

After another short time of silence David said, "We really had a good time together today, didn't we, Daddy?"

"We sure did," I said.

And that was all. David threw the covers back and went quickly to his own room and bed. He was soon sound asleep. But I remained awake for some time. You see, my small son awakened me anew to the importance of taking time to be together as a family.

Our family looked forward to the day at the zoo for a long time. Like many family plans, ours were rescheduled several times. The day was soon over. We were all tired, and we were happy to be at home again. So after a snack no one complained about going to bed. David's words rounded off a happy day with the reminder, "We really had a good time together today, didn't we, Daddy?" And David's mother, who had heard it all, whispered, "It was fun for me also to be together with you and the children today."

Now I know nothing can take the place of such times together. A sense of security, of love, of understanding, and of communication depends upon a feeling of togetherness. When a sense of sharing and togetherness is absent, a feeling of loneliness, strangeness, and lack of love is present.

One of the striking studies issued by those who worked with children who came out of Europe during World War II reveals that the only children capable of rehabilitation to any sense of normalcy after such horrifying experiences were those who had come from homes where they remembered good family times together.

What is togetherness, then? It is taking time for one another. It is chatting around the table or campfire. It is a family walking and running in the woods or park. It is the happiness that comes from doing extra favors for one another. Togetherness is joining hands in some project. It is playing a game that all can join in and enjoy. Togetherness is talking about or praying over a common concern. Togetherness is any word or act that creates the feeling that we are in this thing of living *together*. Togetherness is being able to say at the end of the day, "*We* really had a good time today, didn't we?" If I were beginning my family again, I would try for more togetherness.

I Would Do More Encouraging

If I were starting my family again, I would seek to be freer to express words of appreciation and praise. I reprimanded my children for making mistakes. I sometimes scolded them at the slightest infraction. But my children too seldom heard words of commendation and encouragement when they did a job well or exhibited good behavior.

A minister discussing the topic "If I Had a Teen-ager" says: "I would bestow praise. If the youngster blew a horn I would try to find at least one note that sounded good to my ear, and I would say a sincere good word about it. If the school theme were to my liking, I would say so, hoping that it would get a good grade when it is turned in. If the choice of shirt or tie, or socks or shoes, or any other things met my liking, I would be vocal."

Probably no other thing encourages a child to love life, to seek accomplishment, and to gain confidence, more than sincere praise—not flattery but honest compliments when he has done well.

When Sir Walter Scott was a boy he was considered dull in school. He often was made to stand in the dunce corner with the high pointed hat of shame on his head. He was approximately twelve years old when he happened to be in a home where some famous literary guests were being entertained. Robert Burns, the Scottish poet, was admiring a picture under which was written the couplet of a stanza.

Burns inquired about the author of the couplet. No one seemed to know. Finally a small boy crept up to his side, named the author, and quoted the rest of the poem. Burns was surprised and delighted. Laying his hand on the boy's head he exclaimed, "Ah, bairnie, ye will be a great man in Scotland some day." From that day Walter Scott was a changed lad. One sentence of encouragement set him on the road to greatness. "In praising and loving a child," said Goethe, "we love and praise not that which is, but that which we hope for."

To give encouragement, I would seek to remember the good things my child does and express more freely my feelings of joy, gratitude, and praise for these. I would remember that each day holds many opportunities for encouragement, even in the smallest things. "Judicious praise is to children," writes Christian Bovec, "what the sun is to the flowers." The sun helps the flowers grow in beauty and color. So words of praise are necessary for a child to blossom into a life of loveliness, happiness, and kindness.

Encouragement gives fresh energy, which Dr. Henry H. Goddard says can be measured in the laboratory. At the Vineland Training School, Dr. Goddard used the ergograph which is used to measure fatigue. When someone said to a tired child at the instrument, "You are doing fine, John," the boy's energy curve soared. Discouragement and faultfinding had a measurable opposite effect.

In desiring to bestow praise I would seek to stall scolding words of impatience when my child, through a moment of carelessness, dirties or damages his clothes. Longfellow said, "A torn jacket is soon mended, but hard words bruise the heart of a child." And I think I many times bruised the heart that hurt long after the torn jacket was mended.

I know now that encouragement is a better element of discipline than blame or reprimand. Kind, appreciative words encourage and enable our endeavors. Ruth Hayward in *The Positive Discipline of Praise* relates how she tried to correct her daughter's poor handwriting. It was a constant struggle between them. During the middle of the girl's third year in school there was a change in teachers. After the first day the daughter came home excited about the teacher's saying: "She told me I can write well. I wasn't scared of her. Everybody said she would find something good about us all." From that day her daughter enjoyed school. She became eager to please when she was praised.

I know now that faultfinding, particularly if it is not followed by encouragement, always hurts rather than helps. Faultfinding and criticism rob a child of self-reliance while sincere encouragement builds self-confidence so important to all future life and moves a child on to maturity.

I know now that all of us desire deeply to be appreciated. As the great Harvard psychologist William James said, "The deepest principle of human nature is the craving to be appreciated." And when this need is met by those we love we also will grow in other graces.

I know now that the ability to encourage the hidden resources of a child must be cultivated so that I see not only what the child is now but what the child can be and encourage his becoming. This is to follow Christ who could always see the potential as well as the present response in persons. And no place is this ability more necessary to practice than in the family.

I know now that when we express appreciation in the many small things of life, new love and appreciation grow for one another. If I were starting my family again, I would persist in daily praise.

I Would Pay More Attention to Little Things

I am persuaded today that life is made glad or sad by little things. Little things make or break good relationships, strengthen or shatter a sense of oneness and love, and make us considerate or rude. And if I were starting my family again, I would seek to be more faithful in small things. Most of us can muster enough muscle to manage the major things of life. But we fail in being faithful in the little things. We forget that life is largely made up of the little things and that our faithfulness in the small things determines to a great degree the happiness of the family.

Especially with children, small things wear the garments of greatness. A man, now aged, reminisced about his childhood. "In my childhood days," he said, "my father and mother knew very grave hardship. Yet I recall how whole days of life in our home were glorified and even the hardships seemed light because of my father's graciousness.

"Often early in the morning my father would go out and find the most beautiful rosebud in the rose garden. He would place it at Mother's place to greet her when she came to breakfast. It cost only a few moments of time and a heart full of love. But when he stepped behind her chair as she picked up the rose and gave her his morning kiss, the whole day was glorified. Even the child who had gotten out of bed on the wrong side and come downstairs in a mood to quarrel felt ashamed because life had been touched by the beauty of love expressed in a small but gracious way."

George Eliot wrote, "In a man whose childhood has known caresses and kindness, there is always a fiber of memory that can be touched to gentle issues."

I wish I had known when I began my family how important the small things are. The little acts of kindness and love have a power that we must never underestimate. Just the touch of the hand, a loving smile, a careful compliment, a close caress, can work wonders. A little "thank you" has great reward. An offer to help, a small gift selected with care, can convey affection that warms the heart for weeks. The little words "I love you" and "I'm sorry" enrich both the giver and receiver while their absence allows a coldness to creep in.

So, if I were beginning my family again, I would seek to pay attention to and to love my child through his little hurts. I would wear love on my sleeve in speaking words of love and doing little acts of love. It was too easy to wear my feelings of disappointment and disapproval on my sleeve.

In paying more attention to little things I would seek to remove from my vocabulary such little phrases as "You always" and "You never." I know that these are untrue, that they carry barbs and destroy initiative and drive persons apart.

I would be readier to go a little out of the way to help another, for I know now that it is usually in the small happenings that are unscheduled and that we use for others that have great meaning later. I now realize that when we recall the hurts and helps of childhood, they are usually thoughtless, unkind words that were said in haste, or a moment's pause or touch, that expressed love.

I know now that as oceans are made up of drops of water so happy homes are made of many happy experiences. As mountains are made of many grains of sand, so relationships are made of small grains of goodness in daily life together. And as centuries have their years and years have their days and days are built with hours and moments, it is when we invest the moments with small kindnesses and loving words that the years bring forth a bountiful harvest of beauty and blessing.

Edgar A. Guest wrote a simple and meaningful

prayer that I would make my own if I were starting my family over again. These lines from "Little Things" are expressive of my feelings:

> Although I may not walk with kings,
>   Let me be big in little things.

I Would Seek to Develop Feelings of Belonging

If I were starting my family again, I would seek to instill a strong sense of belonging. A child needs this, and if he does not feel that he belongs in the family and that loyalty and love flow to and from him there, he will very soon find his primary group elsewhere. When a sense of belonging is absent, a feeling of loss and loneliness and lack of love pervades. But when a child feels he belongs in the family and is of real worth there, he enters the world strong, feeling loved and accepted, and with the ability to love and accept others.

I remember times when we felt we really belonged together: the night we were almost blown away in our tent when a terrific storm came up; the early morning hours we searched the shores of Venice, Florida, for sharks' teeth; the nights we lay under the open skies telling stories; and the times we played ball together, cleaned the lawn together, and joined in redoing a room for one of the family. We felt we belonged when we were needed to make something a success. We knew we belonged when we went on a trip or to school, and we all prayed together. We knew we belonged when we were told in a letter or a phone call, "Remember we all love you."

Sometimes, when we are struck with the importance of togetherness and belonging within the family, we set out to plan for things complicated and difficult. Rather than trying things too special I would start by using and strengthening resources that every home already has.

To develop a sense of belonging I would take more time at mealtimes to share experiences and happenings of the day. There is a reason great authors and dramatists center their stories around the table. Yet too often in the family, mealtime, which ought to be relaxing and refreshing, is a hurried ritual from which we rush. It can build a great sense of belonging.

To develop a sense of belonging I'd seek to make bedtime one of the most delightful hours of the day. Bedtime can easily become a time of tenseness because all are tired. In response to the question, What makes you feel you belong to your family? a kindergarten child said, "My mother covers me up and kisses me when I go to bed at night." And a young fellow said, "The happiest and most meaningful moments of my boyhood were the times my mother read to us children before bedtime." I pity the child and family in which the children are hurried and spanked into bed. Bedtime is a great opportunity to build a loving feeling of belonging.

I would seek to make leisure time an occasion to sense we belong together. In a time of more leisure the danger is that each member of the family makes plans to go in different directions and find companions outside the family. I'd cultivate the art of being together and playing together, of playing games or projects in which all can join.

Children are always ready to play games. Often it is the parent who must be given the extra push. Yet as I see it now, use of leisure time is a great opportunity for developing a sense of belonging, of learning together important attitudes of fairness, sportsmanship, consideration, mutual respect and appreciation of one another.

Celebration of birthdays, when the person rather than the gifts is central, creates a sense of belonging. A sense of belonging is built into the child when his opinions are sought and valued and when he is included in the serious and happy experiences of the family. When the family discusses and decides things together a sense of belonging is real.

I would seek to give my child a feeling of

belonging by inviting him to become involved in the responsibilities and work of the family. One writer in pointing out that even small children can do things for others writes, "Work to them is sharing, a sense of belonging, a knowledge that they are individually needed and important to the welfare of the entire family unit." In spite of all the complaining, regular work responsibility, regardless of how small, develops a strong sense of security and belonging, while the child who has no sense of corporate responsibility feels lost at sea.

I know now that no part of child guidance is more important than assuring the child by action and word that he is important to the family and that he has a place in the affection and success of the family.

I know now that when a child senses he belongs to the family he has a security that nothing else can give. He has a stability that can stand against the taunts of the gang and the cries of the crowd. And I know now that it is an almost natural step from knowing that one belongs to a loving, earthly family to the assurance that one belongs to a loving heavenly Father and the family of God.

I Would Seek to Share God More Intimately

If I could begin my family again, I would seek to share God more intimately with my children. By this I mean I would seek, like Christ himself, to choose the ordinary and special things of every day to illustrate the God we have and serve. And I place this deep desire in conclusion because that which I now share must somehow pervade and permeate all the former comments. George McDonald wrote to his wife, "My dearest, when I love God more I love you the way you ought to be loved." And I might add, the more I love God, the more I love each member of my family and community—the way each ought to be loved.

We are not whole persons when we stress only the physical, social, and intellectual. We are spiritual beings. Our lives are linked to the God of creation, and he desires us to be at one with him. When we rest in the confidence of his love and relax in his care, we can face life fearlessly and make the contribution we feel called to make.

In *The Fine Art of Living Together,* the late Albert D. Beaver said that he had sent out questionnaires to seven hundred fifty couples he had married. In answer to the question, "What, in your judgment, is the greatest element for happiness in your home life?" the largest number replied that "it was religion lived daily in the home."

In teaching my child the nature and will of God I would strive to share my faith all day long. I would use the informal settings and unplanned happenings even more than the formal and planned. Rather than discuss abstract theology or impose rigid rules of family worship, I would do more as I rise up and sit down and as we walk by the way. I would pay more attention to the things my child notices and to what concerns him and find in these a natural way to discuss spiritual truths.

A famous British schoolmaster was once asked, "Where, in your curriculum, do you teach religion?"

"We teach it all day long," assured the schoolmaster. "We teach it in arithmetic by accuracy . . . in language by learning to say what we mean . . . in history by humanity . . . geography by breadth of mind . . . handicraft by thoroughness . . . astronomy by reverence . . . in the playground by fair play. We teach it by kindness to animals, by courtesy to servants, by good manners to one another, and by truthfulness in all things."

"Do you talk to them about religion?" the interviewer asked.

"Not much," he said. "Just enough to bring the whole thing to a point now and then."

For the informal settings I would seek to suit my steps to the steps of my child. I would seek more time to stroll by some stream, to pick my Father's flowers, and to see the great Creator in the small as well as the great things of his creation. Today I realize how quickly the child can sense the wonder of God's world—both the natural and spiritual. I would find more time to take sleeping bags in the summer and lie, with my family beside me, under God's heaven and speak of the stars, listen to the noises of nature, the wind whispering in the trees, and the small sounds of unseen creatures. I would provide my child with shelves and drawers on which he could place his trophies and collections.

I would seek to help my child think of God in terms of love, helpfulness, kindness, compassion for the wayward and the Giver of all good things. This is the God of Scripture. He is sometimes pictured, even by parents, as a dreadful deity who works against us.

A four-year-old boy was playing with his sister's mechanical dolls. His mother lay on the divan to take a nap. She was astonished to hear her son say in a thunderous voice, "I'm God. You kids get down on your knees and say your prayers." (They didn't.) "If you don't get down and say your prayers, I'll knock you down," the little fellow said. Then there was a great swoop and all the dolls fell on the floor. What kind of trust and love can a child have in a God who will knock you down if you don't say your prayer?

To share God more intimately, I would notice with my child how God, for a half hour each day at sundown, paints and frames a new picture with the beautiful colors he chooses. I would talk of how he lets the curtains of evening fall while he paints the afterglow of gold in the western windows. I would take time to notice how, in the evening moisture, God makes each leaf look like it has been dipped in the icy liquid of greenness. I would notice, with my child, how God lights the sky with the stars and how he visibly recreates the world during the darkness, making all creation ready for each new day.

I would speak more with my child about how it is God who sends forth the sun, as a strong man to run a race, and as a glowing warmth to evaporate the mist of the morning. I would notice the cluster of butterflies perched on the frayed purple blossom of a thistle.

Then we would look at the lichen-painted rocks, and we would listen to the song of our Father's birds. We would think together how God teaches a bird to line its nest for the comfort of its young and so that those tender and brittle eggs, which we can hardly carry in cotton, lie there without harm until hatched.

We would notice together the charming contrast of land and water and the purity of the newly fallen snow. We'd speak of the silent footsteps of spring when God awakens the seeds, in spite of ice and cold, at just the right time. We'd speak of planting and harvesting and how God also provides spiritually.

So in a thousand ways, I'd seek to use, as our Lord did, the creation to call attention to God's infinite care and love and provision. For I believe that a true understanding of the book of nature when the child is small can help in understanding the book of life later on.

Oh, yes, I would read the Book of Life to my child. But I would seek to relate it more to where my child is. And I would read other books concerning God's care and compassion. And I would seek to show him what God is like in the lives of others. We'd talk with God as a friend and glory in his goodness. I would avoid using God to substitute for my own inadequate discipline by saying things like "God won't love you if you do that."

I would seek to recite a little history each day of God's leading in life and how God delivers physically and spiritually again and again. I would not try to answer every question about the

greatness and the eternal nature of God. I'd rather let my child live in the wonder that there are some things so great about God that even the wisest have never learned of them.

I know now that merely telling my child about God and teaching him a simple form of prayer is a poor substitute for leading him to know God. I now know that parents are to be God's love and that, if the world is to know God and his will, parents are the primary conveyors of his love and will.

I remember a little fellow, frightened by the lightning and thunder, who called out one dark night, "Daddy, come. I'm scared." "Oh, son," the father said, "God loves you and he'll take care of you." "I know God loves me and that he'll take care of me," the small son replied. "But right now, I want somebody who has skin on."

If I were starting my family again, that is what I would want to be—above all else—God's love with skin on. For when the child does not experience God's love, concern, and care from his family, it will be nigh impossible for him to see it or experience it elsewhere in all of life.